Katharina Okon

Teaching English effectively

With special focus on learners' interests

Anchor Academic
Publishing

Okon, Katharina: Teaching English effectively: with special focus on learners' interests.
Hamburg, Anchor Academic Publishing 2013

Buch-ISBN: 978-3-95489-080-4
PDF-eBook-ISBN: 978-3-95489-580-9
Druck/Herstellung: Anchor Academic Publishing, Hamburg, 2013

Bibliografische Information der Deutschen Nationalbibliothek:
Die Deutsche Nationalbibliothek verzeichnet diese Publikation in der Deutschen
Nationalbibliografie; detaillierte bibliografische Daten sind im Internet über
http://dnb.d-nb.de abrufbar.

Bibliographical Information of the German National Library:
The German National Library lists this publication in the German National Bibliography.
Detailed bibliographic data can be found at: http://dnb.d-nb.de

All rights reserved. This publication may not be reproduced, stored in a retrieval system
or transmitted, in any form or by any means, electronic, mechanical, photocopying,
recording or otherwise, without the prior permission of the publishers.

Das Werk einschließlich aller seiner Teile ist urheberrechtlich geschützt. Jede Verwertung
außerhalb der Grenzen des Urheberrechtsgesetzes ist ohne Zustimmung des Verlages
unzulässig und strafbar. Dies gilt insbesondere für Vervielfältigungen, Übersetzungen,
Mikroverfilmungen und die Einspeicherung und Bearbeitung in elektronischen Systemen.

Die Wiedergabe von Gebrauchsnamen, Handelsnamen, Warenbezeichnungen usw. in
diesem Werk berechtigt auch ohne besondere Kennzeichnung nicht zu der Annahme,
dass solche Namen im Sinne der Warenzeichen- und Markenschutz-Gesetzgebung als frei
zu betrachten wären und daher von jedermann benutzt werden dürften.

Die Informationen in diesem Werk wurden mit Sorgfalt erarbeitet. Dennoch können
Fehler nicht vollständig ausgeschlossen werden und die Diplomica Verlag GmbH, die
Autoren oder Übersetzer übernehmen keine juristische Verantwortung oder irgendeine
Haftung für evtl. verbliebene fehlerhafte Angaben und deren Folgen.

Alle Rechte vorbehalten

© Anchor Academic Publishing, Imprint der Diplomica Verlag GmbH
Hermannstal 119k, 22119 Hamburg
http://www.diplomica-verlag.de, Hamburg 2013
Printed in Germany

Table of contents

Introduction – What is the thesis about? 1

1. Motivation and Interest defined 3
1.1 Motivation 3
1.1.1 Behavioural and cognitive theories 4
1.1.2 Arousal theories 6
1.2 Motivation to learn 6
1.3 Intrinsic motivation and extrinsic motivation 7
1.4 Interest 9

2. The importance of interest for language learning in the classroom 11

3. Creating motivational conditions in the classroom 13
3.1 Focus on the teacher 13
3.1.1 Personal characteristics 13
3.1.2. Closeness 15
3.1.3 Classroom management 17
3.2 Focus on the learner 20
3.3 Atmosphere in the classroom 22
3.3.1 A classroom climate free of anxiety 22
3.3.2 A positive classroom environment 23
3.4 Focus on the lesson 23
3.4.1 Materials 24
3.4.2 Activities 27

4. How to increase motivation by including the learners' interests 31
– a research 31
4.1 Aims of the research 31
4.2 The questionnaire 31
4.3 Results of the questionnaire 34
4.4 Evaluation of the results 44
4.4.1 Topics 44
4.4.2 Teachers' personality 45
4.4.3 Methods 46
4.4.4 Media 47

5. The consideration of learners' interests – with a view to the English Lower Saxony Core Curriculum 50

6. Conclusion 52

References 54
Appendices 56

Introduction – What is the thesis about?

Motivation is, without question, the most complex and challenging issue facing teachers today (Scheidecker and Freeman 1999:116, cited in Dörnyei 2007:1).

This quotation covers the importance of motivation for successful language learning in the modern classroom. There are several ways of enhancing students' motivation in the EFL classroom but an important one is to create the lesson on the basis of the learners' interests. Everyone, who looks back on their former school days, might remember that learning was more enjoyable when the topics were interesting and furthermore, when they were handled in an exciting way.

The intention of this paper at hand is to present several ideas of improving the general motivation in the classroom according to the consideration of learners' interests. In addition to that, the current interests of students from German secondary schools and the consideration of the interests in the common English classroom will be presented with the help of a questionnaire.

This paper consists of six main parts. Part one is an overview of the terms motivation and interest. At first, motivation and interest will be defined in their psychological context and in the following these terms will relate to their meaning in the English classroom. It is necessary for the further content of this paper because both of these terms appear frequently throughout the text. In addition to the first part, the second part will mention the importance of incorporating students' interest in the learning classroom.

The third part of this paper will deal with several possibilities of creating motivational conditions in the L2 classroom. Therefore, this paper brings four main factors into focus: the role of the teacher, the role of the student, the atmosphere in the classroom and the lesson itself. In all four sections several ideas will be given how to create a language learning atmosphere that is motivating to the participants of the English classroom.

In addition to the third part of this paper at hand, part four is about a research which is conducted on the basis of the theoretical aspects which are presented in part one, two and three. The intention of the research is, to find out the current interests of students of secondary schools according to different factors of the English learning classroom and furthermore the handling of students' interests in the lessons. Part four includes the aims of the research, the explanation about the questionnaire, the presentation of the results and the evaluation of the outcome. Therefore, the evaluation is based on the four main sections of the questionnaire. These are: topics, the teachers' personality, methods and media.

Part five will deal with the content of the Lower Saxony Core Curriculum and how it considers the students' interests that were represented in part four. The Core Curriculum represents the highest concept to which the English lessons should be structured to. The conclusion will sum up the results of the research and the findings of part five.

1. Motivation and Interest defined

This entire work is based on the psychological term: motivation. Therefore it is important to understand what motivation actually is. Motivation is a concept with many varied aspects. Many authors, psychologists and other professionals have attempted to define motivation, but often the numerous definitions from all the different experts are somewhat unsatisfying because of technical explanations without any practical examples.

In the following Section (Section 1.1), a summary of some of the basic ideas of the term, motivation, are given. This is based mainly on psychological knowledge and concentrates on those aspects deemed relevant to this work. However, this work is written in connection with educational principles, therefore the psychological background is only presented to define the following terms: *motivation, learning motivation, intrinsic motivation* and *interest*.

1.1 Motivation

To understand the meaning and widespread concepts of motivation, it makes sense to give a definition of the word's derivation. Motivation stems from the Latin verb: *movere*. This contains the notion of movement. Motivation is "something that gets us going, keeps us moving, and helps us get jobs done" (Pintrich and Schunk 1996:4). According to Hartinger & Fölling-Albers (2002:16), motivation is usually seen as a process rather than a product. It varies in its intensity and can be dependent on time. For example, on one day a person can be more motivated to go to work than on another.

According to Pintrich and Schunk (1996:4) factors such "as [the] choice of tasks, effort, persistence and verbalization" can have motivation as foundation. To have a reason to behave or to act in a specific way, one has a goal in mind that should be attained. Pintrich and Schunk (1996:4) state that "motivation is the process whereby goal-directed activity is instigated and sustained". Furthermore, motivation involves mental and physical processes of activity. Mental processes are, for example, "actions [such] as planning, rehearsing, organizing, monitoring, making decisions, solving problems and assessing progress" (Pintrich and Schunk 1996:5). Motivation is, more or less, a mental sustainer that helps people to get things done and helps to understand the behaviours of others.

Psychologists call motivation a *hypothetical construct* with no real existence (Hartinger and Fölling-Albers 2002:17), but there is some kind of certainty that there is something inside people that keeps them going in order to achieve a specific goal.
In general, people have an inner motive that explains their behaviour. However, it is important to differentiate between motives, goals and strategies (Brophy 2010: 3). According to Brophy (2010:3), goals are "the immediate objectives of action sequences" and strategies are "the methods used to achieve goals and thus to satisfy motives". Hartinger and Fölling-Albers (2002:17) argue that effort and persistence are the main physical actions of motivation.

Another important aspect, concerning goals, is that they can be reached either in the short-term or in the long-term. For example, it can be a long-term aim when the target is to graduate with high grades or to earn money to build a house Hartinger and Fölling-Albers (2002:17).

1.1.1 Behavioural and cognitive theories

In the history of human psychology, experts have formulated two central theories of motivation: The behavioural and the cognitive theory. Both theories explain possible reasons for the existence of motivation.

Behavioural theories explain that the reason for peoples' motivation "lies in the environment" (Pintrich and Schunk 1996:27). Heckhausen and Heckhausen (2006:5) stated that situational influences include opportunities and possible stimuli that lead to a particular action. The stimuli can be positive or negative. The basic idea of the behaviourists is that drives or needs of an individual are responsible for the actions of that individual (Brophy 2010:3).

Other theories argue that behaviour is caused by reinforcers. Therefore some behavioural theories do not talk about motivation but about control (Brophy 2010:3). This aspect of control relates to the situation at most schools because control by means of reinforcers is the norm. For example, Brophy (2010:3) stated that reinforcers in school are "report card systems, conduct codes, and honor rolls and awards ceremonies". The first two reinforcers mentioned are relevant for the German school system.

Cognitive theories suggest that motivation is an internal process, which can only be observed by "its behavioural products" (Pintrich and Schunk 1996:27). Heckhausen and Heckhausen (2006:3), when explaining cognitive theories of motivation, describes three basic personal elements: implicit motives, explicit motives and universal needs of an individual person. The motives of an individual explain why people behave differently in particular situations. Psychologists infer that people behave differently because of their character, habits and motives, in short: by reason of their personality (Heckhausen and Heckhausen 2006:3).

According to Heckhausen and Heckhausen (2006:4), implicit and explicit motives differ in their level of consciousness. Implicit motives are unconscious because they were learnt during the infancy of an individual and became a confirmed habit (McClelland et al. 1989; cited in Heckhausen and Heckhausen 2006:4). Explicit motives, on the other hand, are conscious and, through verbalization, present self-perceptions of competence, values, goals, affects and norms (Heckhausen and Heckhausen 2006:4). Cognitive theories connect the stimuli of the reinforcer to individual motives. A reinforcer will have lower effect if it is seen as worthless (Brophy 2010:3).

In summary, the motivation of a person to achieve an aim seems to be based on situational stimuli, personal preferences and, of course, on the interaction of both aspects. Situational and personal factors can not be isolated from each other. Both motivation theories are crucial for educational interaction. Pintrich and Schunk (1996:27) stated that:
Behavioural theories imply that teachers should arrange the environment so that students can respond properly to stimuli. Cognitive theories emphasize learners' thoughts, beliefs, and emotions.

Therefore, teachers should be aware of motivational factors, so that they are able to influence them positively with the basic goal to enhance learning and performance in terms of what, when and how long a student learns (Pintrich and Schunk 1996:6).

1.1.2 Arousal theories

Another theory of motivation includes such factors as "behaviours, emotions, and other internal mechanisms" (Pintrich and Schunk 1996:44). These are known as arousal theories and emphasis the importance of affective processes. Cannon (1927; cited in Pintrich and Schunk 1996:44) stressed that a particular perception causes an internal response and aroses emotions that cause certain behaviour.

Physical or mental behaviour, in terms of motivation, can be manifest if there is an optimal level of arousal. Arousal is affected by different kinds of stimuli, for example, novelty, ambiguity, incongruity and surprise (Pintrich and Schunk 1996:45).

Arousal theories are also important to take into consideration when attempting to encourage a motivational atmosphere in the classroom. Pintrich and Schunk (1996:46) stressed four main ideas when applying arousal theories in the classroom:

> 1. maintain student motivation at an optimal level;
> 2. avoid periods of boredom and high anxiety,
> 3. incorporate novelty and incongruity into teaching and student activities and
> 4. develop in students' positive emotions about learning rather than uncertainty.

1.2 Motivation to learn

Learning motivation is not only an essential question in pedagogical psychology, but also in the every day life at school: What drives a student to learn something new? The term, learning motivation, deals with this central question. Krapp (1993:188; cited in Hartinger and Fölling-Albers 2002:32) defines learning motivating in the following way: "Basically learning motivation describes those structures and processes that elucidate the existence and the effects of learning and accordingly of the learning action".

However, from a more formal educational point of view, it is possibly more relevant to deal with learning that is purposeful and intentional (Brophy 2010:12). It is not, however, surprising that learning motivation includes the same basic concepts as motivation in general does: The personal and the situational determinants, action, effect and results (Hartinger and Fölling-Albers 2002:33). According to the theory of learning motivation, it is relevant that a learner connects these aspects to his or her own expectations (Hartinger and Fölling-Albers 2002:33). Brophy (2010:12) summarized this theory as follows:

Motivation to learn is primarily a cognitive experience involving attempts to make sense of the information that an activity conveys, to relate this information to prior knowledge, and to master the skills that the activity develops.

To help understand the complexity of learning motivation, Brophy (2010:12) describes two basic causes: On the one hand, motivation to learn is based on the "general disposition" of a learner and, on the other hand, motivation depends on the situation. General disposition is the extend of a person's willingness to acquire knowledge whereas learning motivation, concerning the situational aspect, happens only if the student sees some importance of the activity or if she/he is interested in it (Brophy 2010:12).

1.3 Intrinsic motivation and extrinsic motivation

There are two main forms of motivation that vary in their cause of action. If someone acts for their own reasons, he or she can be said to be intrinsically motivated. This motivation has an internal cause, for example, if a student works persistently on a task because she/he finds it enjoyable (Brophy 2010:12). This behaviour is not based on "explicit rewards or other external constraints" (Pintrich and Schunk 1996:258). Extrinsic motivation, on the other hand, is the result of external stimuli like rewards or punishments.

Which motivational type, however, guarantees better learning? Formal school education itself seems to foster extrinsic motivation, for most pupils, if only because school attendance is compulsory. In addition, other extrinsic elements of school are marks and school reports. However, this does not exclude the existence of intrinsic motivation at school (Hartinger and Fölling-Albers 2002:37).

Hartinger and Fölling-Albers (2002:37) differentiate between two forms of intrinsic motivation that can be found in the classroom. On the one hand, motivation could be enhanced through activities, and, on the other hand, intrinsic motivation occurs because of the topic that is dealt with. But through which motivation do students reach a better learning goal – extrinsic or intrinsic? According to Hartinger and Fölling-Albers (2002:37), intrinsic learning is normally more successful than extrinsic learning, because students learn more deeply. In addition, Pintrich and Schunk (1996:258) state:

Students who are intrinsically motivated engage in activities that enhance learning; they attend to instruction, rehearse new information, organize knowledge and relate it to what they already know, and apply skills and knowledge in different contexts.

Extrinsic learning is based, to a greater or lesser degree, on cursory learning strategies like simplified repetitions. This might infer that better learning does not only involve factual knowledge, but the comprehension of the item (Hartinger and Fölling-Albers 2002:38). It is important to enhance and encourage the learners' intrinsic motivation to create a successful learning atmosphere in the classroom (Several ideas of how to do so are discussed in Section 3.).

As previously mentioned, intrinsic and extrinsic motivation are two types that exist somewhat separately from one another; but extrinsic rewards can have a negative influence on intrinsic motivation. This fact has to be recognized in the language learning classroom as well as in the general classroom. Pintrich and Schunk (1996:274) argued that all findings of different researches are similar with regard to the problem of extrinsic influences. Pintrich & Schunk give the following example: Julia likes painting. After school she sits at her writing desk at home and paints colourful pictures. Now, she is intrinsically motivated to paint, because she likes it. One day, her mother comes in and asks Julia to paint a picture. Julia will get sweets for it when she finished the painting. Every time Julia paints a picture she receives sweets from her mother. Now, Julia is external motivated, because she is painting for the reward (sweets). In the following days, Julia is not given sweets for her paintings, so she stops painting pictures. In this case, the reward had becomes a controlling factor (Pintrich et al. ibid.). When the mother stopped offering any rewards, Julia lost her motivation to paint.

Every learner might know this: One learns much better and more intensively if learning is fun and interesting. Therefore it is not unimportant to create an enjoyable learning environment by connecting learning with positive activities or by including interesting contents. (Section 3 expands on this important point.)

1.4 Interest

As with motivation, the term of interest exists in general language use and might be connected with, for example, hobbies, what one likes to do, a topic that one wants to know more about, in short 'something that one is interested in'. Pedagogics uses *interest* as a term of motivation that refers to the learning object in the classroom. Autonomy is a central attribute of interest and infers that behaviour, which is brought about by extrinsic motivation, does not necessarily include interest (Hartinger and Fölling-Albers 2002:43). For this reason, interest can be seen as an aspect of intrinsic motivation.

As mentioned in Section 1.3, in order to motivate pupils, it is necessary to foster their intrinsic motivation. This is possible if the teacher arouses the interest of the learner. Regarding activities, Brophy (2010:185) created some factors that will help to arouse this interest:

- Type of activity bases on the learner's temperament (active vs. quite tasks)
- Fun and enjoyment
- Relevance
- Activities that brings the feeling of empowerment or creativity
- Meaningful and satisfying
- identification

Adapted from Brophy (2010:185)

Those mentioned aspects rely, for the most part, on personal perceptions, dispositions and emotions. In general, it is differentiated between individual and situational interest (Brophy 2010:185).

Hartinger and Fölling-Albers (2001:46) distinguish between individual and situational interest by stating that individual interest is persistent, whereas situational interest relates to current motivation regarding an objective. It then follows, that individual interest could be involved into the L2 classroom if the lesson or rather the curriculum is structured around special topics, for example hobbies (Brophy 2010:186). Teachers might find it much easier to have some influence on the situational interest of pupils because "that is generated mainly by environmental conditions" (Krapp et al., cited in Pintrich and Schunk 1996:302).

As previously mentioned, individual and situational interests are two separate concepts. However, Krapp (1998, cited in Hartinger and Fölling-Albers) states that there might be a possibility that situational interest can develop into a steady individual interest. Brophy (2010:186) created a model of the development of interest, involving four steps:

1. Triggered Situational Intent
2. Maintained Situational Intent
3. Emerging Individual Interest
4. Well-Developed Individual Interest

During the first step, the interest arises through a specific condition or, in the classroom, by means of a meaningful activity (Brophy 2010:187). The second step will follow if the situational interest is enhanced by several factors. Brophy (2010:187) mentioned factors like: support from the teacher or from other students, personal involvement and if the topic is important to the person, she/he will want to gather more information about it. The next step of development is achieved as soon as the learner "starts to generate questions" and will emerge, for example from the activities (Brophy 2010:187). According to Brophy (2010:187), interest will be well-developed if the learner sees the objective or the activity as the reward and if she/he will want to further engage in different forms of it.

2. The importance of interest for language learning in the classroom

To ensure a better learning in the language classroom the intrinsic motivation of the students should be supported and encouraged (see Section 1.3). This section will deal with the importance of incorporating the student's interests into the L2 classroom. In the following paragraphs the main advantages will be presented.

According to Hidi and Berndorff (1998:75, cited in Hartinger and Fölling-Albers 2001:82) interest and instrinsic motivation are linked to each other. People who are interested in a specific object or activity spend more time and pay a great deal of attention to it as to something that is uninteresting to them. The outcome of this is that interest has a general effect on student's achievement (Hartinger and Fölling-Albers 2001:83). Additionally, Krapp (1992:21) stated that learning achievement can be attained by cognitive factors as intelligence and non-cognitive factors as motivation and interest.

In several researches Schiefele (1991, cited in Hartiner and Fölling-Albers 2001:85) found out that one will give careful thought to an object and triggers associations if one has prior knowledge of this specific object or if there are emotional connections to it. In contrast, further studies (Schiefele 1998, cited in Hartinger and Fölling-Albers 2001:85) proved that learning without any interest is often cursory. For example: If a learner reads a text about sports and she/he is unintcrested, she/he will not understand it as well as an interested reader would do. Furthermore, the uninterested learner will know the context only by repetitions and an interested learner internalised it just while she/he is reading the text (Hartinger and Fölling-Albers 2001:85). In summary, interest influences learning mainly in its intensity.

Another study carried out by Helmke (1993, cited in Hartinger and Fölling-Albers 2001:88) corroborates the fact that pleasure in learning also influences the students' achievement positively. Helmke (1993) found out that pupils with low pleasure in learning showed behaviour as general avoidance to participate in the lessons and to do homework. If the worst comes to the worst, the deficits resulting from avoidance might cause anxiety to produce language (Hartinger and Fölling-Albers 2001:88).

There are different possibilities to create a language lesson in terms of the students interests (will be discussed in Section 3). But at this point it shall be mentioned that an interesting lesson enhances education in different ways. Hartinger and Fölling-Albers (2001:92) stated that one important factor is the encouragement of autonomy. The autonomy of the learners can be fostered by involving them as often as possible into lesson-based decisions, for example, it might be very interesting for the learners if they have somewhat influence on the learning object (Hartinger and Fölling-Albers 2001:92). Hartinger and Fölling-Albers argued that students who have the possibility to participate autonomous in class will be more interested in the subject itself.

3. Creating motivational conditions in the classroom

Before motivation can be effective in the EFL classroom elementary conditions are needed which are created by the teacher, the learners and their environment. Thus, this section brings the motivational influences of the teacher and of the group in the language classroom into focus. The environment in the classroom is another important factor that will be dealt with. Depending on whether these specific conditions exist, motivation or demotivation will be the result.

3.1 Focus on the teacher

Usually, the common language lesson is designed by the teacher. She/he decides how the lesson is structured, which materials and methods are used, which topics are discussed and when the lesson starts and accordingly ends. In a nutshell, the teacher plays the leading role in the classroom.

The behaviour of the teacher influences the learning process and the motivational conditions of the students for the most part. Dörnyei (2007:31) stated that a self-conducted survey showed that "the participants considered the teacher's own behaviour to be the single most important motivational tool". Concerning the motivational effect of the teacher, Harmer (2007:20) stated that "one of the teacher's main aims should be to help students to sustain their motivation".

Now, what are the behavioural factors of the teacher that effect students' motivation? The following paragraphs will present the main three aspects of teacher behaviour that have great impact on the general student motivation. These are: *The teachers' personal characteristics*, *teacher closeness* and *classroom management* (Dörnyei 2001:35).

3.1.1 Personal characteristics

As mentioned above, the behaviour of a teacher in class is one of the most effective factors for creating motivation in the language learning classroom. It is understood that an unmotivated teacher is unable to affect the learners' interaction in the classroom positively. An unprepared and boring teacher will not create a motivating atmosphere in the classroom.

It is necessary to help the students to be interested throughout a longer period in the subject, so that they will acquire the learning aim (see Section 2). Csikszentmihalyi (1997, cited in Dörnyei 2001:177) stated that popular teachers have the most influence on the students' development, because they behave in a way that is motivating to the students. Outstanding characteristics of a popular teacher are enthusiasm and emotions. Enthusiastic teachers are interested in their own subject and are able to infect the students with their interest by showing dedication and passion "that there is nothing else on earth they would rather be doing" (Dörnyei 2001:178).

In order to motivate the students to learn, the teacher must be aware of the value of the curriculum's content and the methods she/he will use for implementing it (Brophy 2010:214). Then, the teacher might be able to explain why this specific content of the lesson is important for the students.

According to Brophy (2010:215), most students will learn better if they understand the value of activities and the importance of learning English, for example: "Speaking English enriches life in many ways" (Dörnyei 2007:33). Of course, a teacher would only clarify the importance of the subject authentically if she/he believes in it as well. Concerning this theory, Csikszentmihalyi (1997:77, cited in Dörnyei 2001:178) stated the following:

If a teacher does not believe in his job, does not enjoy the learning he is trying to transmit, the student will sense this and derive the entirely rational conclusion that the particular subject matter is not worth mastering for its own sake.

Now, if a teacher wants to enhance the general motivation in the EFL classroom he needs to share her/his own interest with the students (Dörnyei 2007:33). According this, the teacher should not to be too emotional regarding to the own subject or to a specific topic of the lesson. It might be funny for the students if the teacher, for example, begins to cry while dealing with *Romeo and Juliet* or if she/he cannot control her/his anger (Dörnyei 2007:33). If a teacher is not able to deal with own emotions she/he might make a fool of her-/himself and he probably will lose the students' respect (Dörnyei 2007:32).

A further factor of the teachers' personality is: competence. According to this, Pintrich and Schunk (1996:167) stated the following:

Perceived model competence aids observational learning because students are more likely to attend and pattern their actions after models who perform successfully than those less competent.

According to Pintrich and Schunk (1996:167), the factor competence depends, consequently, more on the function of a role model. Of course, competence of a teacher would not necessarily cause motivation (Pintrich and Schunk 1996:168) but students might take a competent teacher more seriously than one, who performs poorly.

3.1.2. Closeness

Teacher closeness represents a further factor of creating motivational conditions in the classroom. This factor surely bases on the teacher's behaviour as well. As the knowledge transferring part, the teacher needs to care about the learners' development and goal-oriented success (Dörnyei 2007:36). For achieving this, the teacher should not only be the 'transferring factor' but a supporter and helper concerning the learning process. If a teacher does not care about the students, they will quickly sense it by means of the teacher's absence. Regarding this Dörnyei (2007:34) assumed that:

The spiritual (and sometimes physical) absence of the teacher sends such a powerful message of 'It doesn't matter!' to the students, that everybody, even the most dedicated ones, are likely to be affected and become demoralised.

Summing up, not caring about the students will affect a demotivating atmosphere and probably will damage the teacher-student relationship. However, Dörnyei (2001:34) creates some ideas about showing learners that the teacher is interested in their learning process:

- Offering concrete assistance
- Offering to meet students individually to explain things
- Responding immediately when help is requested
- Correcting tests and papers promptly
- Sending learners copies of interesting articles
- Allowing students to call you at home when they have a problem
- Being available for overtime

Adapted from Dörnyei (2001:34)

Those ideas show generally what a teacher can do to show interest in the academic progress of the students. However, all of those aspects contain the extra need of time. Therefore, it is not really surprising that some teachers might not put into praxis especially the last two ideas of Dörnyei (2001:34).

Furthermore, it comes as no surprise that a good relationship between the teacher and the learners does not only depend on an academic interaction but on a personal level (Dörnyei 2007:36). That means in general, that the teacher cares for students "as real people" Dörnyei (2001:36). It is surely not easy to build rapport with all students taught by a teacher. A main reason for this difficulty might be the extra time that is needed to develop the relationship to the students.

However, there are three basic aspects which foster a good relationship between the learner and the teacher: "Acceptance of the students, ability to listen and pay attention to them and availability for personal contact" (Dörnyei 2007:37). Dörnyei stated that a main factor of accepting the students is to be free of prejudices. Thereby, it is necessary to have a positive attitude in general without thinking in stereotypes.

Furthermore, a good teacher would pay attention to the students needing help. Concerning Dörnyei (2007:37), it is of course nearly impossible to spend a lot of time listening and talking to all the students while teaching language skills. However, Burden and Raffini (1995:224,1996:182, cited in Dörnyei 2007:38) created some possibilities for teachers in what way to show the students that 'I'm interested in you!' without much effort. In the following a few selected bullet-points will be mentioned:

- Greet students and remember their names
- Smile at them
- Notice interesting features of their appearance
- Show interest in their hobbies
- Recognise birthdays
- Move around in class
- Send notes/homework to absent students

Adapted from Dörnyei (2007:38)

Those ideas of paying attention to the students enhance the general relationship between teacher and learners. The aspects do not only represent interest in the students' person itself but include the factor acceptance that was mentioned beforehand.

Availability is a further aspect that is important for a good teacher-student relationship and that is also difficult in its realisation because the teacher needs extra time. Teachers might use the chances to meet their students in the playground, at school events, or at school-lunch (Dörnyei 2007:38). Furthermore they could show availability by giving their email address and telephone number to their students, for example if the students need any support.

Summing up, it is really necessary for the relationship between teachers and learners that the teachers "indicate mental and physical availability" (Dörnyei 2007:39). If the students know that the teacher cares for them and if they feel "supported and valued, they are far more likely to be motivated to learn" (Harmer 2007:21).

3.1.3 Classroom management

When it is about *classroom management* one might guess of organising and planning a lesson. But the meaning of *classroom management* regarding to the teacher's roles also includes the activities of setting rules and discipline students. Those factors influence the students' motivation in another main manner. The next paragraphs will deal with *classroom management* regarding the implementation of group norms. The motivational factor *classroom management* in terms of materials and activities will be explained in chapter 3.4.

It is an incontrovertible fact that there is a better learning-atmosphere in a cohesive learner group (Brophy 2010:23). A cohesive learner group is characterized by a friendly cooperation between the particular students. There are no single groups or strong cliques but "one which is 'together'; in which there is a strong 'we' feeling" (Dörnyei 2007:43).

According this, a further function of the teacher is creating a learner group whose cohesiveness is on a high level. There are different possibilities and ways of forming a collective group (Dörnyei 2007:44). As a teacher, it is expedient to begin her/his 'investment' into the learner group as early as possible, for example when a new course starts (Dörnyei 2007:43). Ideal for this situations are activities in which the class members get to know each other.

Another way of enhancing the group cohesiveness is maintaining the contact and interaction of the students by using methods like pair work, group work or project work (Dörnyei 2007:44). Therefore, the students get the chance to help and support each other, to work on a same task, to find a good solution and to present the outcome of the group together. Lesson experiences like that will foster the cohesion for the most part (Dörnyei 2007:100). Concerning Dörnyei (2007:44), the teacher could put students who do not know each other very well into 'competition groups'. Especially competitions will keep the particular group members together and develop the relationships between the learners.

Another idea of creating a cohesive learner group, which is not mentioned by Dörnyei, might be the chance of spending time together, for example on a school trip or one-day excursions. The main advantage of this is that the students do not only share their time on the basis of learning because a school trip always involves freetime. They will get the possibility to get to know each other outside of the learning conditions.
To maintain a cooperative group of students, it is necessary to create group norms in the learning classroom (Dörnyei 2007:45). Making learning in the classroom enjoya-

ble and free of fear there are special rules needed which have to be considered. At the risk of establishing rules there might be the effect of demotivation. Therefore, new rules have to be accepted by the learners (Dörnyei 2007:46).

Concerning rules-integration into the classroom Dörnyei (2007:46) created "an explicit norm-building procedure":

1. formulating norms
2. justify their purpose
3. discuss them with the group
4. let learners formulate further norms (and discuss them)
5. agreeing on the final 'set of class rules'

Adapted from DÖRNYEI (2007:46)

The final 'set of class rules' should include all participants of the EFL classroom and there should be rules for everyone and not only for the students. Creating rules for the teacher as well, for example "Finish class on time" or "Give notice of a test" (Dörnyei 2007:46), might bring motivation to consider the rules in general about. An important point of rules in the classroom is that everybody is willing not to break them. For remembering those daily, the accepted rules can be fixed, for example, in form of a poster (Dörmyei 2007:46).

Especially the teacher, as the leading participant, has to pay attention to the 'set of class rules', because if the teacher does not take the rules seriously the students might not, either (Dörnyei 2007:47). Considering the rules, which are created by the students and the teacher, a good and motivational learning atmosphere will increase (Dörnyei 2007:45).

However, if there are students who break the rules, how should a teacher behave without reducing motivation in the classroom? Firstly, it is necessary to notice the disregard of the rules (Dörnyei 2007:49). Rule-breaking behaviour should never be ignored, because if the teacher ignores it once or twice, the teacher may lose her/his credibility and furthermore the 'set of class rules' will lose its importance. Secondly, the best way of discipline students without lowering motivation could be "to leave it to the students themselves" Dörnyei (2007:47). Regarding to the importance of the group manner, the group of learners has to handle with problems like these, precisely because such situations may enhance adhesiveness. But the main reason for letting the group cope with students who break the rules, is that the group itself particularly has the most power to put pressure on somebody (Dörnyei 2007:48).

However, if a group do not feel up to handle such situations it should be the teacher who has to discuss the erratic behaviour (Dörnyei 2007:48). For saving the general motivation the teacher needs to make very clear, that the behaviour of a students is not accepted, but not the student oneself (Dörnyei 2007:48).

3.2 Focus on the learner

At the beginning of a new language course different learner come together, everyone with various expectations, everyone with a different level of competences and of course some might be motivated or even demotivated. Concerning the institution school, most of the learners study English as a foreign language in primary and secondary school. Harmer (2007:12) stated that students learn English because it is on the curriculum. First at least they may not have a specific reason to learn this language such as learners who learn it for instance for business, for international communication (e.g. travelling) or for operating in a target-language community (Harmer 2007:11). So, the students participate in the course, because they somehow have to. Therefore, motivation has become an important part of the modern language classroom.

Concerning Riemer (1997:77) foreign language acquisition is naturally an individual progress, which is subject to the general human qualifications. Furthermore, Riemer stated that language acquisition relies on the input that learners assimilate. In summary, it depends on the learner how much input she/he is able to assimilate and in how far the learner is able to interact (Riemer 1997:77). In addition, every single learner is influenced by her/his own personal factors and particularly how she/he learns in general. According to this, Nunan (1998:170) created four different types of learners:

> 1. The 'concrete' learners
> 2. The 'analytical' learners
> 3. The 'communicative' learners
> 4. The 'authority-oriented' learners

Adapted from Nunan (1998:170)

The types of learners that Nunan (1998:170) mentioned above differ basically in their preferences regarding to learning. Their motivation will be on the highest level if the lesson is created according to their preferences. The four types of learners will be explained in the following:

The 'concrete' learner will be motivated if the lesson includes games, pictures, films, CDs, working in pairs and doing activities outside the classroom (Nunan 1998:170).

The 'analytical' learner in contrast prefers working alone, reading books, working on task given by the teacher and studying rules like grammar (Nunan 1998:170). The 'authority-oriented' one is similar to the 'analytical' learner because she/he also likes learning grammar, but the main point is that this learner likes to do everything the teacher says (Nunan 1998:170). At last, the 'communicative' learner tends to practise language through authentic materials such as listening to native speakers and talk to other people in the other language (Nunan 1998:170).

Another idea is, to distinguish between extroverted and introverted learners. Riemer (1997:59) stated that in our western society the statement is common that extroverted language learners are the most successful ones. They achieve better communicative competences by reason of their unresisted interaction with other speakers. In contrast, introverted speaker are often determined to avoid mistakes. The consequence of the self-effacement is that their interaction in language is low (Riemer 1997:59). Studies (Suter 1976 and Busch 1982, cited in Riemer 1997:59) supported the fact that extroverted learners have more speaking-competences than introverted.

Depending on whether learners are extroverted or introverted, the classroom interaction in general will be high or low. Especially introverted students tend to speak rarely, in order to avoid negative evaluation through the teacher (Riemer 1997:60).

Therefore it is important to create a classroom-atmosphere which is free of anxiety. This point will be discussed in the following section (Section 3.3).

3.3 Atmosphere in the classroom

Dörnyei (2007:40) found out with the help of a research that the classroom climate is the second most important motivational factor, just after *teacher's behaviour*. According to this, classroom climate and the classroom's environment play a major role. The following paragraphs will deal with these factors.

3.3.1 A classroom climate free of anxiety

A goal-oriented learning calls basically for a good atmosphere in the classroom so that every learner is allowed to make mistakes (Dörnyei 2007:41). First language learning plays a decisive role by reason of the high anxiety of producing language faulty. It might be no rarity that learners avoid talking in other languages in the classroom as they are afraid of the negative feedback from the teacher or from the class members (Dörnyei 2007:41). This is a main problem, because language learning naturally bases upon speaking. Therefore it is essential to lower the general language anxiety in the EFL classroom.

A main aspect for a climate free of anxiety is, of course, how the students behave among each other. As it was mentioned in section 3.1.3, a cohesive learner group includes a supporting and nice cooperation. There is no laughing about each other or put-downs in such learner groups but respect and trust (Dörnyei 2007:41). If students feel safe in their group they will probably take risks to make mistakes (Dörnyei 2007:41).

Another factor that has influence in learners' language anxiety is the teacher. With the help of a good relationship (see Section 3.1.2) to the students the fear to speak will be lowered conspicuously. In addition, the teacher has to make clear that making mistakes is absolutely fine because the learners are in a process of learning (Dörnyei 2007:42).

A very important point that reduces anxiety effectively and increases motivation is the use of humour. Regarding this, Dörnyei (2007:41) stated the following:

The main point about having humour in the classroom is not so much about continuously cracking jokes but rather having a relaxed attitude about how seriously we take ourselves.

Humour in this case is an essential factor for creating an enjoyable atmosphere. It is very necessary for the students' language acquisition that they recognize that learning a language can be fun.

3.3.2 A positive classroom environment

A learning motivating atmosphere in the classroom includes the whole environment of the class. In general, the teacher and the students spend day-by-day in one special classroom. Therefore, it is also important for a motivating atmosphere to create a relaxing and inviting environment in the classroom. Especially decorations like posters, flowers or plants or other nice objects influence the classroom environment positively (Dörnyei 2007:41). Also furniture as bookshelves, suitable desks and chairs enhance the learning conditions as well as learning materials, for example models, maps, books, pencils, etc. Regarding the learning materials, the teacher should pay attention to the compatibleness relating to the curriculum (Brophy 2010:24). Furthermore, classrooms could be featured with (learning-) games that can be used during free-time periods as long breaks.

Dörnyei (2007:42) mentioned the importance of involving students to create the classroom according to their taste. Students would feel more comfortable if the classroom is created by their ideas and preferences. Having control about the environment of the classroom, for example the paint of the wall may encourage the motivation in another way (Dörnyei 2007:42).

3.4 Focus on the lesson

In the following paragraphs the focus will be on materials and on activities. Materials and activities are factors of the lessons that are dealt with basically. The section of materials distinguishes between published and authentic materials. According to those, selected materials will be described in their motivational content and influence on the students.

The section of activities will present ideas of implementing activities in a motivational way into the EFL classroom.

3.4 1 Materials

Teachers often are spoilt for choice when it is about using materials in the classroom. In terms of enhancing motivation, the choice of a material is as important as the use of it. The next paragraphs deal with several selected materials regarding their motivational effectiveness. Therefore, the materials are separated into published and authentic ones (Gower, Phillips and Walters 2005:77).

Concerning Gower et al. (2005:77) textbooks, as published materials, are used for the most part in the classroom. They are commonly student's textbooks that are used during the lessons and the student's workbook that focus more on individual work. Furthermore, the common textbooks contain materials like videos or CDs that are matched with the textbooks' content (Gower, Phillips and Walters 2005:77). Audio and visual materials make the textual structure and content of the books more interesting and focus on reading and listening comprehension.

Regarding the motivational foundation, there are advantages and disadvantages of using those textbooks in the language classroom: Textbooks are "a ready-made source" of language work including activities, grammar, vocabulary, pronunciation and skill acquirement (Gower, Phillips and Walters 2005:77). In addition to that, the levels of the texts are suitable for the special ages of the students. Furthermore, Gower et. al stated that using a textbook in class does not need as much preparation or organisation as other materials do. However, the teacher has to mind when using the book. It is not indicated to use a textbook for the whole lesson, day by day (Gower, Phillips and Walters 2005:78). According to this fact, Gower et al. (2005:78) state:

When planning your lessons, think about which parts of the coursebook could be omitted, which could be used and which need supplementing with activities and materials from other sources.

According to Gower et. al (2005:78) using textbooks in class without adding other materials cause disadvantages and problems, for example: students will be bored of the onesided use of material, books often do not suit the interest of the students (mainly related to the topics of the texts), following the structure of the coursebook as a teacher may cause uncreativeness, demotivation and boredom during planning and holding a lesson and leads to the problem, that the teachers go trough the textbook without understanding what they are doing and why they are doing so.

In summary, textbooks are important sources for the classroom interaction but it should be seen critically, in particular relating to the students needs and interests and even to the difficulties of exercises and texts. "The success of a coursebook depends to a large extent on how well it is used by the teacher" (Gower, Phillips and Walters 2005:78).

Other significant published materials are videos. Commonly, they are used in class to train listening and speaking (pronunciation) skills (Gower, Phillips and Walters 2005:81). Videos produced for the EFL classroom are usually coordinated to the textbooks, so that exercises and texts of the book fit together with specific sequences of the video (Gower, Phillips and Walters 2005:81).

According to Lonergan (1994:5), videos include the advantage of stopping, considering, or to having a look again at an earlier passage. A possible break into a linear progression is another basic advantage of videos. This form of media is "intrinsically interesting to the language learners" and he or she wants to watch the film, even if their comprehension is limited (Lonergan 1994:5). If there is enough interest a teacher "can create a climate for successful learning" (Lonergan 1994:5). Furthermore, videos have a communicative value, because they present full situations of communication. According Lonergan (1994:5), the language learner can see the ages of the characters, their sex, their relationships, their dress, social status, what they are doing and their mood and feelings. Therefore, video materials are very authentic. A further advantage, stated by Lonergan, is that moving pictures are good for an imagination and for remembering aspects afterwards.

However, there are negative aspects of using videos in the English classroom. Videos are related to other materials somewhat expensive (Gower, Phillips and Walters 2005:81). Furthermore, a lesson based on a video needs to be well prepared. The teacher has to choose the right sequences and the suitable tasks and she/he has to think about when using the video. An important aspect is that the film should fit into the lesson's structure, more precisely "You will have to make sure, as with all supplementary materials, that you select carefully so that the video is well-integrated with the other elements of your lesson" (Gower, Phillips and Walters 2005:81). The value of students' motivation will get lost if teachers do not keep these advises in mind. As with other materials, showing videos too often will cause a lack of interest and motivation.

CALL (Computer Assisted Language Learning) is another method that is used in the EFL classroom. The several software is commonly produced for educational practice and include numerous ways of training language, for example: "Matching words and sentences, reconstructing a text or filling in gaps with words" (Gower, Phillips and Walters 2005:82). Some software are equipped with exercises based on games and simulations, that increase fun and with it motivation (Gower, Phillips and Walters 2005:82). Furthermore, a lot of programs have feedback, so they are able to give answers if an exercise is solved correct or wrong. Hence, learners can work with the programs by their selves or even in pair work. There are some possibilities to use CALL differently, as Gower, Phillips and Walters (2005:81) state:
The whole class can be set the same task if the computers are networked […]. In this way time spent using computers can be a useful integrated stage of a longer lesson or a series of lessons.

Using CALL in class is also motivating for students who have difficulties on handwriting (Gower, Phillips and Walters 2005:82). Especially those students will welcome to do their written exercises on the computer.

However, this popular material also hides problems of demotivation. According to Gower et al. (2005:82) the teacher has to get straight that not all students are familiar with learning software and computers in general. It is important that the teacher is informed about their skills beforehand because some students might need some help (Gower, Phillips and Walters 2005:82).

Authentic materials differ from published material insofar that they are not designed for the EFL classroom and are not based consequently on special language levels. Gower et al. (2005:81) stated:
Anything a native speaker of English would hear or read or use can be described as authentic: theatre programmes, newspapers, magazines, poems, songs, brochures, information leaflets, menus, news broadcasts, films on video – the list is endless.

By reason of the authenticity, the levels of skills are missing. Therefore, the teacher has to choose the material that should be used in class advisedly (Gower, Phillips and Walters 2005:82). According to Gower et. al (2005:83), it is necessary for the teacher to know the needs and interests of the learners to assure the basic motivation of the students. Due to the use of authentic materials the teacher's knowledge about the general language-level of the students is especially important, too, because exercises that are too difficult or actually too easy will bring boredom, excessive demand and demotivation about. In general, authentic materials are motivating and interesting for the students because they include 'real' language that is used in the Anglophone countries (Gower, Phillips and Walters 2005:83).

An outstanding advantage of authentic materials is that the learners get the chance to deal with day-to-day situations, for example ordering a meal in a restaurant by reading the menu or discussing news that they have seen on a video or have read in a newspaper.

3.4.2 Activities

The first step of using activities in the EFL classroom is the presentation of it. The presentation of an activity is important because depending on whether it is presented the teacher will "whet the students' appetite" (Dörnyei 2007:80).

Regarding Dörnyei (2007:78) "the motivational introduction of an activity fulfils at least three further functions". Basically, they are: *the explanation of the purpose of the task, the students anticipation* and *the strategies that are needed for the activity.*

Furthermore Dörnyei (2007:79) argues, that it is a main problem that students just do the task because the teacher says so. Therefore, it might be no rarity if students ask themselves 'Why should I do this task? – aside from a good mark or avoiding trouble with the teacher'. So, it must be firstly the business of the teacher (concerning activities) to explain the purpose of the given task (see Section 3.1.1). In addition, it is helpful for the students if the teacher points out what the difficulties of the activity are (Dörnyei 2007:80) .

While presenting the task, the learners will be more interested in it, if the teacher connects the activity to personal aspects of the students so that the student can identify with the topic and accordingly with the activity (Brophy 2010:185). 'The topic and I' will enhance the intrinsic motivation of the students and also effect the students' awareness of the task's purpose (Dörnyei 2007:80). Motivating students doing a task also includes presenting it with enthusiasm and maybe humour (see Section 3.3.1). Therefore, the teacher could involve the students by making guesses or predictions about the task (Dörnyei 2007:80). A task presentation is always interesting for the learners if the teacher depicts it, for example with pictures.

A further aspect of enhancing motivation through activities is the involvement of everyday situations. Stedtfeld (cited in Solmecke 1983:316) stated that activities based on daily life topics and experiences are very motivating to the students, because they have to deal with problems or situations that are real. In addition, the value of the activity is higher when it relates to a real situation, for example students are elaborating a role play in which they have to demonstrate the interaction between a costumer and a waiter in a restaurant (Brophy 2010:169).

Enhancing the motivation of the learners relates in particular to the development of their language acquisition. If they recognize that they are doing well in achieving the goal-oriented learning aim, for example through the feedback of the teacher, the intrinsic motivation of the learners will increase automatically (Brophy 2010:190). Optimizing the intrinsic motivation of the language learners by developing competences can be gained through learning activities. According to Pintrich and Schunk (1996:277), activities are fun for the students when the intrinsic motivation in learning may increase, so that they will achieve the different language skills as writing, speaking and reading (see also Section 2).

Concerning this matter, Pintrich and Schunk (1996:277) assumed four special concepts that are essential for enhancing motivation by using activities in class. Those four are: *challenge, curiosity, control* and *fantasy*. The following paragraphs include the explanation of the concepts regarding activities and how the teacher can implement them into the lesson.

The first important point of motivating activities is the level of tasks. On the one hand students are easily bored if the tasks are too easy and on the other hand difficult activities might effect reluctance and with it demotivation. The best activities are those which levels of difficulty are intermediate but rise with the developed competences of the learner (Pintrich and Schunk 1996:277). Pintrich and Schunk (1996:277) stated that students might set new goals with increased competences.

For creating and involving suitable activities the teacher has to be aware of the students' different competences. To attend to the individual differences, it is convenient to split the learner into groups regarding their level of competences (Pintrich and Schunk 1996:279). So, every group could deal with the right intermediate activity.

However, students who are assigned to the 'group of lower competences' might be unmotivated by seeing themselves as the weakest link. It is almost significant to keep the motivational factor of the coherent group belonging in mind (see Section 3.1.3).

Furthermore, *curiosity* plays a decisive role in using and presenting activities. Pintrich and Schunk (1996:277) argue that students' curiosity is particularly high if and only if the "information or ideas are discrepant from their present knowledge or beliefs" because those might seem "surprising or incongruous". Then, learners are willing to get the information and resolve the lack of knowledge. Therefore, teachers should integrate surprise into the activities (Pintrich and Schunk 1996:279).

As it was mentioned in section 3.3, motivation will be enhanced when the students get a part of *control*. This finding is also based on activities in the classroom (Brophy 2010:190). Control by the students might be: having a choice in the form of activities, having a say in how much time they need for an activity and how to present the outcome.

High motivating activities involve *fantasy* as well. Those implicate in particular activities in which students are able to make believes, for example, in terms of simulations or games (Pintrich and Schunk 1996:280). Free-writing activities include fantasy, too.

Often, after the task instruction was spoken out by the teacher, the students sit there without doing anything. For the teachers, this behaviour is sometimes inexplicable because the task was introduced clearly and interesting to the students. One reason that re-emerges over and over is simply (the conclusion) that 'the students did not listen carefully!'. But another reason might be that the students do not know "how to go about completing the task" (Dörnyei 2007:80). Regarding this, the teacher needs to demonstrate important strategies that are needed for working on a specific task. There are different possibilities for presenting strategies, for example by putting oneself in the students' position while presenting the steps or creating a brainstorming with the learners (Dörnyei 2007:81).

The wide range of methods of a lesson like whole class working, solo work, pair work, group work or project work are disregarded in this chapter, by reason of their individual interest basing content. On the one hand there might be some learners who prefer working by their selves for various reasons, but on the other hand there might be learners who like to do activities in groups or with a partner. Every form of method has advantages or disadvantages that are based on individual preferences. This will find regard in Section 4.

4. How to increase motivation by including the learners' interests – a research

4.1 Aims of the research

Interest is a main factor when attempting to enhance motivational conditions in the language learning classroom. In Sections 1, 2 and 3, the importance of arousing the students' interest in the EFL classroom to improve motivation was discussed. Several motivational factors were presented and defined, according to the accepted theories.

To corroborate the theory, and to become aware of the 'real' interests of the English language learners in Hildesheim, it was necessary to conduct a piece of research. Depending on the results, it could be possible to incorporate the needs and interests of the learners into the English lessons. The differences of gender and age will be important for the more practical aspects of the classes.

In order to test the hypothesis: there would be less consideration of students' interests in the most current English classroom, the following piece of questionnaire was conducted. The interest of the students, regarding the *topics*: *teachers' roles*, *methods* and *materials*, are presented, and how far these interests are taken into consideration in the current English classroom is investigated.

4.2 The questionnaire

The research was conducted, using a questionnaire (see Appendix 1 for the questionnaire). This consists of four basic units: students interests related to *topics*, *teachers' personality*, *methods* and *materials*. The particular questions of the units were in the form of multiple choice because of the large sample group (Trochim 2006). Therefore, the data is quantitative. A total of 169 students (83 boys and 86 girls) from years five, six, eight, nine and ten were questioned about their interests regarding the aforementioned aspects. All the participants answered the questions voluntarily and anonymously.

The length of time to complete the questionnaire was approximately ten minutes. In addition, the research was cross-sectional, because it took place at one single period of time. The outcome is based on the current situation at the school. It is possible that the outcome might be different if the survey was conducted at another location (Kromrey 2006:405).

It is also important to say that the results of this research are not necessarily applicable to all pupils throughout Germany. It only gives information about the practical application of students' interests in an English learning classroom in Hildesheim (Kromrey 2006:405).

The structure of the questionnaire is described in the following:

Before completing the questionnaire, the participants were given some information about the research. The particular bullet points, on the questionnaire, included that the answers would be anonymous, how long the questionnaire would take, and that the research was being conducted for the University of Hildesheim.

When analysing the results, it was necessary to find out if there are any differences between the sexes or the ages, concerning the interests of the pupils. Therefore, the students were asked about their gender, their age and what class they attended.

After giving the personal information, the participants were questioned about their general interest in common topics. They had to write down at least three topics. The pupils then had to decide whether they would like their interests to be incorporated into the English lessons. The third question: *How interesting are the following topics to you?* is a multiple choice question and includes different topics that are dealt with in the English classrooms in secondary schools of Lower Saxony.

Some topics, for example, *school in England, John is moving* or *future*, were selected from German textbooks. The topics are structured into four basic sections because it is necessary to discover what groups of topics are interesting or, of course, uninteresting for the students.

Question four and question five deal with the current learning content of the students' English class. The students had to state the actual topics of their English lessons and were asked to evaluate them in terms of how interesting they found them.

The next part of the questionnaire: *teachers' personality* consists of two main questions. The first one is a multiple choice question. The learners had to evaluate several facets describing the teacher's personality. They were also asked what facet is the most important one for them.

The third part of the questionnaire: *interest in methods*, is similarly structured to the fourth part: *interest in media*. The first step was to find out what methods or media were liked by the students and which were disliked. Furthermore, the learners stated the method and the medium that they prefer most. The students were asked to give reasons for their choices. Finally, the last multiple choice questions were related to the actual situation in the English classes, for example: *How often do you use the different methods/media in class?* The students had the choice of the following possibilities: *very often, often, seldom, never* and *I don't know*.

The following problems were considered before handing out the questionnaires:

The students might not take it seriously so that the answers would not be valid. Another problem could be that the participants are influenced by people such as their teachers, or external factors such as time. The questionnaire was given out at the beginning of the lessons. Therefore, it might have been a problem to find teachers who are willing to spare time from their lesson. It was also possible that some pupils would not have time to complete the questionnaire.

The following problems were considered after handing out the questionnaires:

A main problem was that at least 2 classes were influenced by their teacher because she/he shouted out the answer. Of course the aim was to check how many students could remember the current topic of their English class because if not the result will testify to an uninteresting topic. Furthermore, a few questionnaires were not completed because the teacher stopped the students.

4.3 Results of the questionnaire

Question 1 investigates the students' level of interest in different topics. The students were asked to state at least three topics, from their daily life, that they found interesting. See Table 1 for the four most mentioned topics:

Topics	Answers
Sports	96
Computer	47
Music	45
Friends	45

Table 1: Students' interest in daily topics

In all classes, *sports, computer, music* and *friends* are the most stated topics. The topic, *sports*, was of more interest to boys (73), and more girls than boys mentioned *music* (32) and *friends* (36).

For Question 2, the pupils were asked if they would like their interests to be taken into consideration in the classroom. Q2 consisted of three pre-formulated answers: *Yes; I don't mind;* and *No, not really.* See Table 2 for the results of Q2: *Would you find it good if your English class dealt with these topics?*

pre-formulated answers	number of answers
Yes	108
I don't mind	43
No, not really	7
No answers	11

Table 2: Students' opinion about covering the topics they are interested in, in the English classroom

As can be seen from Table 2, 64% of the students would find it good if the topics that they had mentioned in Q1 were integrated into the English lessons. Only 4% of the students were not interested in covering the topics mentioned in Q1.

Question 3 covered a range of different topics. The students were asked to evaluate these topics in terms of their personal interest. The range includes the following scales: *interesting, okay* and *uninteresting*. For the results of Q3, see Table 3: *How interesting are the following topics to you?*

Topics	interesting	okay	un-interesting
London	55	90	21
Traditions in England	22	67	77
School in England	49	77	42
The USA	112	48	9
School in the USA	69	78	20
States of America	48	79	40
Family P. goes to the Zoo	24	45	100
John is moving	13	47	108
Sammy's Family	10	43	114
Clothes	81	71	16
Holidays	121	42	6
Jobs	99	60	10
Technique	63	58	47
Future	106	56	5
Food and drinks	57	71	39
My favourite sports	84	68	16
My pet	69	59	41
My Family	84	60	25
My daily life	93	54	22

Table 3: Level of interest, depending on the topics

As can be seen from Table 3, answers were mixed. However, on the basis of the given results it can be said that there are obvious differences in interest between the main four sections of topics (see 4.2), which are described in the following:

A comparison of the given results according to the section of Cultural Studies (*London, Traditions in England, School in England, The USA, School in the USA* and *States of America*) shows that topics of the USA are in general more interesting to the students than topics about England.

47% of the stated answers, related to the topics of England, are found in the category *okay*. In particular, the topic *Traditions in England,* seems uninteresting (77 answers) to the students and only 22 students found it interesting.

The results of the answers given for the topic *The USA* are very clear. Here, 112 from 169 students stated that this is an interesting topic and only 9 of them were not interested.

The next section of the given topics is based on experiences of fictional people (*Family P. goes to the Zoo, John is moving* and *Sammy's Family*). 64% of the questioned students found all three topics uninteresting.

The topics: *clothes, holidays, jobs, technique, future* and *food and drinks,* were based on general topics. As can be seen from Table 3, answers were fairly mixed. However, most of the given answers were found in the sections of *interesting* and *okay*. The topics *holidays* (121 answers) and *future* (106 answers) were of particular interest to the students.

The last four topics: *my favourite sports*, *my pet*, *my family* and *my daily life,* focus on personal aspects of the learners' lives. 49% of the students were found in the scale of *interesting* and 36% of them voted for *okay*. One exception is the topic, *my pet*. Here, the evaluation was mixed. The following answers were given: *interesting*: 69 *okay*: 59 *uninteresting*: 41.

In terms of the comparison between the answers given by the boys and the girls, that is, gender specific, there are no significant differences. Only the answers for the topics *clothes, technique* and *my favourite sports* show noticeable differences. As can be seen from Table 4, girls were more interested in *clothes* than the boys, and the boys found the topics *technique* and *my favourite sports* more interesting.

Topics	interesting		okay		un-interesting	
	f	m	f	m	f	m
Clothes	49	32	28	43	8	8
Technique	11	52	37	21	37	10
My favourite sports	29	55	43	25	12	4

Table 4: Gender-related differences in the interest of topics

However, there are, of course, age-based differences. This becomes apparent by the *further topics* that were given (see Appendix 3 for the particular Tables). In particular, year five and year six stated topics which were not mentioned by the other classes, for example, *school* and *playing*. Year eight and year nine are somewhat similar in relation to the students' interests. In addition to *sports*; *computers*; *friends* and *music*, *TV* and *different countries* are popular. The students of year ten, in contrast, are more interested in topics like *the other sex, love and hate, motorbikes, politics* and *news*.

Question 4 deals with the current situation in the English classroom concerning topics. The students were asked to write down the actual topics of their English lessons. In addition, the students had the possibility to make a tick in a given answer box if they did not know the topic.

Question 5 is connected to the previous question. Here, the students were questioned about their personal opinion: *How interesting do you find the topic?* There were four answer boxes given with the following grading: 1: *very interesting*, 2: *interesting*, 3: *uninteresting*, 4: *Does not interest me at all* and 5: *I don't know*. In addition, the students had the possibility again to tick an answer box if they were not sure about their answer. More than a half of the students remembered the current topic of their English class. As can be seen from Table 5 the following topics were mentioned (Q4) and evaluated (Q5):

Topics	very interesting	interesting	un-interesting	Does not interest me at all
Grammar	5	18	3	2
USA	9	11	-	-
Technology	2	8	6	2
Australia	3	24	4	4
Future	2	1	-	-
Sports	-	4	1	-

Table 5: Level of interest of current topics in the English classrooms

38 of the questioned students could not give an answer to Q4. Another 22 of the students stated different topics that are not included in Table 5. As can be seen from Table 5, students found most of the topics *interesting*.

Question 6 investigates the students' interest in the personality of a teacher. They were asked to evaluate several facets of a teacher's character in terms of importance. The following grading was used for this question: *very important, important, I don't care* and *unimportant*. Table 6 represents the results of Q6: *I'm searching for the perfect English teacher. What characters are important to you?*

she/he should	very important	important	I don't care	unimportant
be funny	91	59	4	15
know her/his subject	126	37	2	4
be fair	137	27	1	3
be friendly	127	39	/	3
be available	57	81	5	26
be strict	4	29	82	53
be patient	64	81	4	20
be sensitive	48	65	10	44
be consequent	40	71	15	40
be motivating	119	41	2	6
impart the teaching content understandably	139	27	–	2
perform well under pressure	50	62	13	43
handle criticism	80	59	3	26

Table 6: Importance of teachers' character

As can be seen from Table 6, 139 students (from 169) found that the most important point of teachers' character is *imparting the topic understandably*. Other important characters that were evaluated, with more than 100 responses, are: *being fair* (137), *being friendly* (127), *knowing own subject* (126) and *being motivating* (119). Only 4 students found it *very important* that a teacher should be strict.

Other aspects that were mentioned are amongst others: *being cool, having a sense of humour, setting no homework, being helpful, being young, being happy, being always up-to-date* and *playing games with the students*. There were no significant differences between the ages or the genders in the responses to this question.

The answers of question 7: *What factor do you find is the most important one?* are similar to those of Q6.

Question 8 is about a further factor which influences the student's interests in the English classrooms: methodology. First of all, the students were requested to state their preferences concerning methods used in the English classroom. The scale was in form of smileys: ☺:*I like*, ⊖: *neutral*, ☹: *I dislike*. See Table 7 for the results of the following question: *What methods do you like or do you dislike in your English class?!*

Methods	☺	⊖	☹
Teacher talk	24	119	25
Solo work	35	100	34
Pair work	140	24	3
Group work	124	30	15
Project work	102	50	16
Circuit training	52	68	49

Table 7: Students' preferences of methods in their English class

As can be seen from Table 7, pair work is the most popular method. In general, methods that involve contact with other students are really popular. Again, the students' interests in methods do not show any differences, according to gender or age.

In addition, the students were asked about their favourite method in Q9 and about the reason for their decision in Q10. The most stated methods were group work (68), pair work (46) and project work (45). The students who stated group work as their favourite method gave the following main reasons: "Contact, fun and the exchange of information". For pair work, the following answers were given: "Contact, fun, quite and fast exchange of information and better understanding" and the main reason for project work was "the chance of being autonomous". Those students who preferred solo work gave as reasons "better concentration, testing the own knowledge and quietness".

Question 11 deals with the current use of the several methods in the English classroom. The students were asked: *How often do you use the different methods in class?* Q11 covers the same methods stated in Q9. The students gave the following answers (see Table 8), the scale was: *very often, often, seldom, never* and *I don't know*):

Methods	Very often	often	seldom	never	I don't know
Teacher talk	19	60	48	8	24
Solo work	81	69	14	-	-
Pair work	16	81	60	3	6
Group work	13	20	68	60	5
Project work	6	4	49	86	19
Circuit training	5	19	21	103	17

Table 8: Current handling of methods in the English classroom

As can be seen in Table 8, the most used methods in the English classrooms are *solo work* (*very often*: 81), *pair work* (*often*: 81) and *teacher talk* (*often*: 60). Methods seldom used are: *circuit training* (*never*: 103), *project work* (*never*: 86) and *group work* (*seldom*: 68).

The last part of the questionnaire deals with the topic: media, and in how far they are interesting to the students and, furthermore, how often they are used in the English lessons. Therefore, the students were asked, in Question 12, to state their preferences in relation to media. The same grading as in Q8 was used: ☺:*I like*, ☻: *neutral*, ☹: *I dislike*. The results of the question *What media do you like or do you dislike in the English class?* are presented in Table 9.

Media	☺	⊖	☹
The English textbook	47	89	30
Work sheets from your teacher	59	77	30
CDs in English	104	47	16
Films in English	134	22	10
Working with the blackboard	47	95	25
Working with my exercise book	44	95	28
Working with the workbook	83	72	12
Pictures	98	59	10
Overhead projector	52	84	31
Learning programmes on the Computer	106	40	20
English journals	30	68	67
Poster	73	68	25

Table 9: Students' preferences of media in their English class

Table 9 shows that *films, learning programmes on the computer* and *CDs* are the most popular media in the English learning classrooms. A total of 134 students chose *films* and gave the following reasons for their choice: "Fun, a better comprehension, a better learning of pronunciation and films are interesting". The students stated the same reasons for *CDs*. Further statements of the students show, that they believe that they will learn English much better by listening to authentic material than to their teachers.

The last question (Question 15) refers to the use of the selected media in the current English lessons. The students were asked to answer Q15 according to the following scale: *very often, often, seldom, never* and *I don't know*. See Table 10 for the given answers of Q15 (*How often do you work with the following media in your English class?*):

Media	Very often	often	seldom	never	I don't know
The English textbook	92	45	14	13	1
Work sheets from your teacher	66	72	20	-	3
CDs in English	21	83	51	4	2
Films in English	1	8	44	102	8
Working with the blackboard	53	67	30	11	2
Working with my exercise book	48	75	26	9	5
Working with the workbook	47	59	32	23	2
Pictures	5	44	84	23	6
Overhead projector	7	32	67	49	8
Learning programmes on the Computer	7	7	21	121	5
English journals	-	1	11	146	5
Poster	1	14	54	83	11

Table 10: Current handling of media in the English classroom

As can be seen from Table 10, the most used media are: *the English textbook* (*very often*: 92), *worksheets* (*very often*: 66), *working with the blackboard* (*very often*: 53), *working with my exercise book* (*very often*: 48) and *working with the workbook* (*very often*: 47). *CDs* (83) are also often used in the English classrooms. Media with less use are *English journals* (*never*: 146), *learning programmes on the computer* (*never*: 121), *films* (*never*: 102) and *poster* (*never*: 83). 84 students stated that *pictures* were seldom used.

4.4 Evaluation of the results

In this section the results of the research will be evaluated. The interests of the young research participants will be compared with the topics taught in the English classes. As with the questionnaire, the evaluation is structured into the four sections: *topics*, *teachers' personality*, *methods* and *materials* (see 4.2).

4.4.1 Topics

The section, *topics*, is divided into three main parts (see Appendix 1). Question 1 and 2 relate to the present interests of the students. The students were asked to write down at least three topics they are interested in. As can be seen from Table 1, the topics mentioned most were *sports*, *computer*, *friends* and *music*. In every questioned class those topics were the most interesting ones.

In order to include the interests of the pupils, in the language classroom, the teacher needs to be aware of age-based differences. As can bee seen from Table A-G (see Appendix 3 for the particular Tables), lower classes are more interested in topics of their daily life, for example: school, friends, shopping, hobbies and so forth. In higher classes, the learners also mentioned similar topics but, in addition to the four main topics, *sports, computer, music and friends*, *feelings* play an important role. The older the students the more they are interested in 'grown-up topics' like *love*, *news* and *politics*. It might be, therefore, somewhat difficult to motivate pupils from year five or six by 'talking about the next presidential elections'.

The results of the section *topics* might not be surprising because it somehow natural that the interests will differ the older a child or a teenager is. However, the essential outcome of the questionnaire is that there are four main topics which were mentioned most in all classes – regardless of which year. The reason for this result might be that those topics are not age-based. It is most likely that a pupil from year five is as interested in sports as a student from year ten, they will have friends and, most probably, computers. They will most definitely have feelings. But, as mentioned above, it is more unlikely that the student from year five is deeply interested in, for example, love.

More than a half 64% (see Table 2) of the questioned students stated that they wish to deal with topics, in which they are interested, in the English classroom. This result is not really surprising because one's motivation to learn will be higher when the subject matter is about something that is interesting to her/him (see Section 2).

The results of Question 3 show that the students are somewhat interested in Cultural Studies. But, as can be seen from the given results, the students are more interested in the United States of America than in England. The greater visibility of the USA in the media could be one possible reason for this result.

Furthermore, it is obvious that all topics based on stories of fictional characters are not of great interest to the pupils. On the one hand there might be the reason that the students did not understand what was meant by the topics. On the other hand, a reason might be that they could not identify with those fictional people. In summary, a student might not be interested in 'John is moving' because she/he does not actually know who John is. One would suppose that the pupils live with her/his parents and will not move out in the coming years.

The students found the last four topics of the schedule (see Table 3) interesting. Those topics relate to the daily life of the students. They surely can identify with topics like *my favourite sports* and *my daily life* (see Section 3.4.2). Furthermore, the students found the general topics like *technique*, *holidays* and *future* also interesting. Therefore it is motivating to students if the teacher includes such topics in the English lessons.

As can be seen from Table 5, 131 of the students could remember the current topic of their English class. 66 of them found it *interesting* and 21 students found it *very interesting*.

4.4.2 Teachers' personality

In Section 3, the importance of the teachers' personality was explained. Therefore it was necessary to include this important point in the questionnaire to find out what facets of the teachers' character are important to the students. The results are now discussed.

As can be seen from Table 6, the students voted the factor, *impart the teaching content understandably,* as the most important one, even more important than: *being fair*, *being friendly* and *being funny*. This result might be somewhat surprising, but this factor is a really important function of a teacher. But teaching comprehensibly might also include using appropriate teaching materials, being friendly, being patient and so forth.

Characteristics such as *being fair, being friendly, knowing one's own subject* and *being motivating* were chosen by more than 100 students. The first above mentioned factors relate directly to the teacher-student relationship, which will be, naturally, improved by means of a friendly and fair interaction (see Section 3.1.2). The 126

The outcome of this result (126 responses of knowing *one's own subject*) is that the competence of the teacher is a very important factor to the students. The further factor of *being motivating* shows the importance of including the students in the lesson and making any topic interesting. As already mentioned in Section 3, the motivational factor will, in general, improve the learning of the students.

4.4.3 Methods

As previously mentioned (see Section 4.4), the section on methods include the results of the students' interest in several methods and, on the other hand, the results show the current use of these in the English classroom.

As can be seen from the results, the students prefer working in pairs, groups or by doing a project. These forms of methods include contact and interaction between the students. Especially interesting were the reasons given for preferring these methods. The following reasons were given by the students: "…because I can work with my friends.", "It is better to work with others than working by myself.", "It is more fun when working with others.", "…the more people, the more information.", "…because I can discuss in a group.", "In a project you can choose your own topic.", "It is fun to reach an outcome together.", "…we can help each other.", and so forth.

As can be seen from the students' answers, they like to have some influence on the task, for example, choosing a topic (see Section 3.4.2). However, statements like "helping each other" show that they wish to have the opportunity to obtain help form their classmates, if necessary. In summary, the given answers relate to the importance of "being together, working together and reaching an aim – together".

From the participants' responses *solo work* and *teacher talk* were evaluated for the most part (*teacher talk*: 119, *solo work*: 100) as *neutral* (see Table 7). A reason for this, concerning *solo work* and *teacher talk*, might be that these are common in the English lessons.

When comparing what methods students are interested in with how often these methods appear in the current English classrooms, the results show that *teacher talk*, *solo work* and *pair work* are the most common three methods. *Group work* is seldom used and *project work* and *circuit training* do not seem to appear in the English classrooms. In summary, two of the three popular methods, that is group work and project work, are *seldom* (68 responses) or even *never* (86 responses) used. This means that the students interests in interacting with others, discussing with others, having influence on activities, helping each other, and so forth, are somewhat disregarded. Even *circuit training*, a method where students can work for the most part autonomously, is ignored in the current English lessons.

4.4.4 Media

As can be seen by the above results from the questionnaire, the students prefer modern media such as *learning programmes on the computer*, *films* and *CDs*. A reason for this might be that the students today are very familiar with these media. As the results from question 1 shows, 47 students spent their free-time on their computers.

Another reason might be the fact that computers, films or CDs are somewhat relaxing for them. The given answers of the students support this statement: "because films are fun", "I don't have to write anything", "films are 'chilling'", "When we work on computers I can surf through the internet", "I don't need to get my exercise book out of my bag when listening to CDs", "listening CDs is easy", and so forth. Even students from year five prefer such materials, but when they have to give reasons for their preferences they often could give no answers.

The rarity of use of modern media, in the English classroom, might be a further reason for preferring, in particular, films and using computers. As can be seen from Table 10, there is virtually no use of films and computers in the most English lessons. Films and/or computers in the language classroom should not be used just for pleasure, but should be connected with learning aims and activities, but attempts should be made to include them in the lessons (see Section 3.4.1). Possibly because these media are seldom used, the students will not know that using films, for example, often includes connected writing or reading tasks.

It is also noticeable that those media which are used quite often were evaluated as being *neutral*, especially the following ones: *the English textbook* (*neutral*: 89, usage: *very often*), *worksheets from your teacher* (*neutral*: 77, usage: *often-very often*), *working with the blackboard* (*neutral*: 95. usage: *often-very often*) and *working with my exercise book* (*neutral*: 95, usage: *often – very often*). The participants found media used frequently not interesting but also not uninteresting. This result indicates more of an acceptance of those media.

As can be seen from the results, students prefer media like pictures and posters. Students who voted for these materials gave the following reasons: "Creating posters is fun, because I can be creative.", "I can learn much better with pictures." and "It is exciting!". In general, posters and pictures are very visual media with often have a motivating effect. They are motivating because they include, amongst others, the four aspects described by Pintrich and Schunk (1996:277): challenge, curiosity, control and fantasy (see Section 3.4.3). Creating a poster is also very motivating for the students, not only because it encourages autonomy (see Section 2), but also creativity.

English journals are somewhat unpopular among the students. However, they are not used in the current English classrooms. A reason for not using them might be the high language level because they are authentic material. In addition, the level of difficulty might be also the reason for unpopularity.

In summary, the results show that most of the students are contented with those materials that are actually used in the English learning classrooms. However, the students' motivation could be improved by using modern materials such as *learning programmes* (e.g.: CALL) or *films* more often.

The results show that the English textbook is used very often (92 students gave this answer). This indicates that the textbook is the material used most frequently. The second most used materials are the worksheets (66 responses).

In conclusion, the results of the questionnaire show that the interests of the students are considered to some extent. The current use of methods and materials is in need of improvement to bring their use in accordance with students' interests. The students are more interested in methods which foster social competences and in modern materials. However, in the English lessons under discussion, traditional materials like textbooks and the blackboard are still the most used media.

5. The consideration of learners' interests – with a view to the English Lower Saxony Core Curriculum

The English Lower Saxony Core Curriculum covers the educational standards, which the students of secondary schools in Lower Saxony should acquire. Therefore, it is necessary to train certain competences so that students will achieve the language learning aim of the curriculum. The Core Curriculum represents the instructions for successful English lessons with the intention that all learners of the secondary schools in Lower Saxony will acquire the same knowledge. By means of the very important role, parts of the Core Curriculum will be analysed in terms of the consideration of the students' interests' that were found out with the help of the questionnaire (Section 4).

The English Core Curriculum contains amongst others the part: *Creating an English lesson with reference to the Core Curriculum* (Niedersächsisches Kultusministerium 2006:8). This part of the curriculum represents the students' interests by reason of the following content:

In the first instance, the curriculum points out the importance of treating the learners individually by considering their individual level of knowledge and competences. This aspect was not researched in Section 4 but treating learners as individuals will be of interest to the students. The importance to pay attention to students' individuality was discussed in Section 3.2.

Additionally, the Core Curriculum refers to the importance of creating the English lessons as authentic as possible. As can be seen in Section 4.3 (Results of the questionnaire), main reasons, given by the students, for preferring films were based on the context of authenticity. The students stated that they will learn much better if they listen to 'real' language.

A further important point of the curriculums' statement of creating an English lesson successfully refers to the importance of creating conditions in the classroom, in which students can make mistakes (see Section 3.3.1).
A further section of the English Core Curriculum covers the term of *methodical competences* (Niedersächsisches Kerncurriculum 2006:22). Different methods of

improving it are stated in the curriculum. The following paragraphs will bring the methods of *interaction*, *media* and *learning organisation* into focus.

An outstanding result of the questionnaire is the students' preference to work in groups and pairs (see Table 7). This result finds attention in the above mentioned section of the curriculum. Furthermore, the section: *media* covers the students' wish to work with learning programmes in the English lessons (see Table 9).

As can be seen from the results of the questionnaire (see Table 7), the students are interested in working together over a certain period of time, for example, working on a project. In addition, it is important for the students to be autonomous while working and they like to have the chance of making choices (see 4.3 for the students' statements). Those three mentioned terms of interest are considered in the Core Curriculum as well (Niedersächsisches Kerncurriculum 2006:23).

In summary, the English Core Curriculum consults learners' interest in several terms. The outcome of this is: If teachers relate to the content of the curriculum, the English lessons will be in most parts motivating to students.

6. Conclusion

In conclusion, the intention of this paper at hand was it to focus on the general improvement of language learning in the English classroom. There are several ways of imparting knowledge or adapting students' competences, for example with the help of different kinds of methods or media. However, developing language skills can only be successful if the students are willing to learn the language. Accordingly, it should be the teachers business to bring the learner to the subject and to motivate them to participate in the English classroom over a certain time.

This paper presented the terms of motivation and interest according to the language lesson. The psychological content of section one was important to understand the internal human processes of motivation and interest. For being motivated, a person needs basically a specific goal and furthermore she/he has to be aware of its value. But motivation can also occur by several stimuli such as stirring up curiosity or by being interested in something. Consequently, the psychological knowledge about getting somebody to do something can be used in the language lesson.

Interest is a factor that stimulates motivation strongly. One way to increase the students' motivation is to deal with the learners' interest in the L2 classroom. As can be seen from Section 2, researches support the fact that students will learn more successful if the learning object is interesting to them. The essential condition, before integrating interest, is that the teacher is aware of the students' interests. On the basis of this, a questionnaire (see Section 4) was given out to students.

The results of the questionnaire represent the students' interests, and whether these are considered in the current English lessons. In the following, the outstanding results of the questionnaire will be presented.

General outstanding outcomes of students' interests were:

> - Stories of fictive people are uninteresting (see Table 3)
> - The most important factor of the teachers' role is that the teacher has to present the learning object as understandably as possible (see Table 6)
> - Students want to work in pairs and groups and they are very interested in doing projects (see Table 7)
> - Students favour modern media like films and learning programmes (see Table 9)

General outstanding outcomes of the L2 classroom situation were:

> - Current topics of the English lessons are interesting (see Table)
> - Usual methods are: solo work, teacher talk and pair work (see Table 8)
> - Usual media are: in the first instance: the textbook and furthermore: the blackboard and worksheets from the teacher (see Table 10)

The results of the questionnaire were also interesting for the teachers of the questioned classes. After the research particular teacher wanted to know what answers were given by the students. This example shows that teachers are interested in the students' preferences according to the lesson.

Furthermore, the Core Curriculum was proved in its interestingness according to the results of the research. The fact is that the content of the English Lower Saxony Core Curriculum depends for the most part on the presented interests.

In summary, there is room for improvement according to the consideration of students' interests in the current English lessons. Modern media is what is requested and working with other students is wanted. However, there are indications that the English lessons will be more innovative in the coming years because a few students stated that their teachers use whiteboards in the English learning classroom.

References

Brophy, J. (2010): *Motivating Students to Learn.* New York: Routledge.

Dörnyei, Z. (2001): *Teaching and Researching Motivation.* Harlow: Pearson Education Limited

Dörnyei, Z. (2007): *Motivational Strategies in the Language Classroom.* Cambridge: Cambridge University Press.

Gower, R., Phillips, D., and Walters, S. (2005): *Teaching Practice. A handbook for teachers in training.* Oxford: Macmillan Education.

Harmer, J. (2007): *How to teach English.* Harlow: Pearson Education Limited.

Hartinger, A., and Fölling-Albers, M. (2002): *Schüler motivieren und interessieren. Ergebnisse aus der Forschung. Anregungen für die Praxis.* Rieden: Julius Klinkhardt.

Heckhausen, J., and Heckhausen, H. (2006): *Motivation und Handeln*: Heidelberg: Springer Medizin Verlag.

Krapp, A., Prenzel, M. (1992): *Interesse, Lernen, Leistung. Neuere Ansätze der pädagogisch-psychologischen Interessenforschung.* Münster: Aschendorff Verlag.

Kromrey, H. (2006): *Empirische Sozialforschung.* Stuttgart: Lucius & Lucius Verlagsgesellschaft mbH

Lonergan, J. (1994): *Video in Language Teaching.* Cambridge: Cambridge Language Teaching Library.

Niedersächsisches Kultusministerium (2006): *Kerncurriculum für die Realschule Schuljahrgänge 5-10. Englisch.* Hannover.
Nunan, D. (1998): *Language Teaching Methodology. A textbook for teachers.* National Centre for English Language Teaching and Research, Macquarie University, Sydney: Prentice Hall.

Pintrich, P. R., and Schunk, D. H. (1996): *Motivation in education. Theory, research, and applications.* New Jersey: Prentice-Hall, Inc.

Riemer, C. (1997): *Individuelle Unterschiede im Fremdsprachenerwerb. Die Wechselwirksamkeit ausgewählter Einflußfaktoren.* Hohengehren: Schneider Verlag.

Solmecke, G. (1983): *Motivation und Motivieren im Fremdsprachenunterricht.* Paderborn: Ferdinand Schöningh.

Trochim, W. (2006): *Research Methods. Knowledge Base.* Received September 25, 2010 from http://www.socialresearchmethods.net/kb/guideelements.php

Appendices

Bullet points
- survey in context of an academic assignment
- time of survey: ca. 10 minutes
- anonym, data will be treated as strictly confidential

☐₁ female   ☐₂ male

Year: _____

Age: _____

1. Give at least 3 topics from your daily life, in which you are interested!

1. _____

2. _____

3. _____

2. Would you find it good if your English lesson dealt with these topics?

☐₁ Yes
☐₂ I don't mind
☐₃ No, not really

3. How interesting are the following topics to you?

	interesting	okay	un-interesting
London	☐₁	☐₃	☐₄
Traditions in England	☐₁	☐₃	☐₄
School in England	☐₁	☐₃	☐₄
States of America	☐₁	☐₃	☐₄
School in the USA	☐₁	☐₃	☐₄
Staates of America	☐₁	☐₃	☐₄
Family P. goes to the Zoo	☐₁	☐₃	☐₄
John is moving	☐₁	☐₃	☐₄
Sammy's Family	☐₁	☐₃	☐₄
Clothes	☐₁	☐₃	☐₄
Holidays	☐₁	☐₃	☐₄
Jobs	☐₁	☐₃	☐₄
Technic	☐₁	☐₃	☐₄
Future	☐₁	☐₃	☐₄
Food and Drinks	☐₁	☐₃	☐₄
My favorite sports	☐₁	☐₃	☐₄
My pet	☐₁	☐₃	☐₄
My Family	☐₁	☐₃	☐₄
My daily life	☐₁	☐₃	☐₄

characters are important to you?

she/he should	very important	important	I don't care	un-important
be funny	☐₁	☐₂	☐₅	☐₃
know her/his subject	☐₁	☐₂	☐₅	☐₃
be fair	☐₁	☐₂	☐₅	☐₃
be friendly	☐₁	☐₂	☐₅	☐₃
be available	☐₁	☐₂	☐₅	☐₃
be strict	☐₁	☐₂	☐₅	☐₃
be patient	☐₁	☐₂	☐₅	☐₃
be sensitive	☐₁	☐₂	☐₅	☐₃
be consequent	☐₁	☐₂	☐₅	☐₃
be motivating	☐₁	☐₂	☐₅	☐₃
impart the topic understandably	☐₁	☐₂	☐₅	☐₃
perform well under pressure	☐₁	☐₂	☐₅	☐₃
handle criticism	☐₁	☐₂	☐₅	☐₃
Other:	☐₁	☐₂	☐₅	☐₃

7. What factor do you find is the most important one?

_____

8. What methods do you like or do you dislike in your

4. What is the current topic of your English lesson?

☐₀ *I don't know → → carry on with question 6*

☐₁ _____

5. How interesting do you find the topic? Tick the right answer!

☐₀ *I don't know*

☐₁ very interesting

☐₂ interesting

☐₃ uninteresting

☐₄ Does not interest me at all.

6. I'm searching for the perfect English teacher. What

English class?

😊 I like   😐 neutral   ☹ I dislike

	😊	😐	☹
Teacher talk	☐₁	☐₂	☐₃
Solo work	☐₁	☐₂	☐₃
Pair work	☐₁	☐₂	☐₃
Group work	☐₁	☐₂	☐₃
Project work	☐₁	☐₂	☐₃
Circuit training	☐₁	☐₂	☐₃
Others:	☐₁	☐₂	☐₃

9. What method do you like best? _____

10. Why? _____

11. How often do you use the different methods in class?

	Very often	often	seldom	never	I don't know
Teacher talk	☐₁	☐₂	☐₃	☐₄	☐₅
Solo work	☐₁	☐₂	☐₃	☐₄	☐₅
Pair work	☐₁	☐₂	☐₃	☐₄	☐₅
Group work	☐₁	☐₂	☐₃	☐₄	☐₅
Project work	☐₁	☐₂	☐₃	☐₄	☐₅
Circuit training	☐₁	☐₂	☐₃	☐₄	☐₅
Others:	☐₁	☐₂	☐₃	☐₄	☐₅

12. What media do you like or do you dislike in the English class?

😊 I like   ⊖ neutral   ☹ I dislike

	😊	⊖	☹
The English textbook	☐₁	☐₂	☐₃
Work sheets from your teacher	☐₁	☐₂	☐₃
CDs in English	☐₁	☐₂	☐₃
Films in English	☐₁	☐₂	☐₃
Working with the blackboard	☐₁	☐₂	☐₃
Working with my exercise book	☐₁	☐₂	☐₃
Working with the workbook	☐₁	☐₂	☐₃
Pictures	☐₁	☐₂	☐₃
Overhead projector	☐₁	☐₂	☐₃
Learning programmes on the Computer	☐₁	☐₂	☐₃
English journals	☐₁	☐₂	☐₃
Poster	☐₁	☐₂	☐₃
Others:			

13. With what medium do you like to work best?

14. Why?

15. How often do you work with the following media in your English class?

	Very often	often	seldom	never	I don't know
The English textbook	☐₁	☐₂	☐₃	☐₄	☐₅
Work sheets from your teacher	☐₁	☐₂	☐₃	☐₄	☐₅
CDs in English	☐₁	☐₂	☐₃	☐₄	☐₅
Films in English	☐₁	☐₂	☐₃	☐₄	☐₅
Working with the blackboard	☐₁	☐₂	☐₃	☐₄	☐₅
Working with my workbook	☐₁	☐₂	☐₃	☐₄	☐₅
Working with the workbook	☐₁	☐₂	☐₃	☐₄	☐₅
Pictures	☐₁	☐₂	☐₃	☐₄	☐₅
Overhead projector	☐₁	☐₂	☐₃	☐₄	☐₅
English journals	☐₁	☐₂	☐₃	☐₄	☐₅

Topics	Answers	
	f	m
Music	5	3
TV	1	1
Sports	8	7
Theme parks	-	1
Computer	-	1
Cars	-	2
Culture	1	1
Drawing	2	-
Clothing	1	-
Friends	9	2
Shopping	1	-
Technique	1	1
Sleeping	-	1
Food	-	2
Traveling	3	-
Lifestyle	1	-
Reading	1	-
Nature	1	-
Politics	1	-
Table C: Year 8		

Topics	Answers	
	f	m
Music	4	-
Sports	6	5
School	2	3
Computer	3	7
TV	1	1
Food	1	1
Shopping	6	3
Stars	-	1
Holidays	-	1
Hobbies	3	2
Mobile phone	1	4
Books	-	1
Animals	2	-
Medicine	-	1
Turkey	-	1
Table A: Year 5		

Topics	Answers	
	f	m
Music	2	-
Sports	4	12
School	2	1
Computer	2	2
Cars	-	1
Food	2	1
Clothing	1	1
Family	1	-
Friends	5	-
Technique	1	-
States of America	2	-
England	2	-
Spain	1	-
Relaxing	-	2
Animals	3	1
Holidays	2	-
Daily Life	1	-
Table B: Year 6		

Topics	Answers	
	f	m
TV	5	2
Sports	3	7
Computer	3	5
Music	3	3
Animals	2	-
Friends	5	2
General knowledge	-	1
Family	1	1
Holidays	-	1
Future	-	1
Cooking	1	2
Shopping	1	-
Stars	1	-
Hobbies	-	4
England	-	1
London	-	1
Theater	1	-
Books	3	-

Topics	Answers	
	f	m
Environment	1	-
TV	-	3
Sports	4	15
Computer	2	12
Jobs	-	1
Clothing	1	-
Hobbies	1	-
Friends	4	3
States of America	7	1
Family	1	1
Having fun	1	1
Parties	-	1
Animals	-	1
Food	-	2
Medicine	1	1
Table E: Year 9		

Topics	Answers	
	f	m
School	2	-
Music	5	6
TV	2	1
Sports	5	8
Computer	3	1
Animals	1	1
Jobs	-	1
Books	1	-
Friends	3	1
Hobbies	2	1
Technique	-	3
Culture	1	5
Politics	1	1
News	-	2
Shopping	4	-
Future	-	1
Family	1	1
Sleeping	-	1
Food	1	1
Table F: Year 10		

Topics	Answers	
	f	m
Films	1	2
Music	8	6
Sports	1	11
Teenager	-	1
Cities	-	1
Computer	-	6
Motorbikes	-	2
Money	-	2
Girls	-	3
Clothing	-	1
Cars	-	1
Friends	10	1
Hobbies	1	1
Technique	1	1
States of America	-	1
Love	10	-
Hate	1	-
Family	1	-
Table G: Year 10		

Made in the USA
Monee, IL
03 May 2026